'70s Chil

Born in 1972, you experienced the birth of new technologies that would change our World forever. Unlike children born from the '90s onwards you remember a world before technology invaded the everyday. You were lucky to have experienced a real childhood; playing in the streets with your friends with days spent making up games from your imagination.

Despite the social and economic unrest that pervaded the decade there were many families enjoying a better standard of living than previous generations. This drove consumerism as more and more families had money to spend on leisure products and activities.

The fabric of Society was changing. The move towards individualism can be seen throughout all areas of life, most notably through music and fashion. The '70s saw the creation of amazing musicians and bands. This grew in tandem with an explosion of new fashion styles reflecting the various sub cultures in society.

The divorce act that passed in the late '60s begins to impact the structure of families. By the end of the decade 1 in 8 families are headed by single parent.

Women's liberation slowly builds momentum. More women chose to stay in the workplace after marriage and children. There are calls in all areas of society towards equality. Despite this it's clear when looking at advertising that this was in no way achieved but instead was the seeds of what would grow into something more significant.

This book takes a peek back in time to all the things you knew and loved as a child of the '70s and maybe some that you have forgotten.

50 YEARS AGO BACK IN 1972

WORLD MAP

World Population

3.8 BILLION

Britain population

56.01 MILLION

2022

World Population

8 BILLION

Britain population

67.81 MILLION

MAJOR WORLD LEADERS

UK- PRIME MINISTER - EDWARD HEATH

US PRESIDENT - RICHARD NIXON

RUSSIA/SOVIET UNION - FIRST SECRETARY OF THE CPSU
LEONID BREZHNEV

SOUTH AFRICA - PRIME MINISTER - BALTHAZAR JOHANNES
VORSTER

ITALY - PRIME MINISTER - EMILIO COLOMBO

WEST GERMANY - CHANCELLOR - WILLY BRANDT

EAST GERMANY - ERICH HONECKER, CHAIRMAN OF THE
COUNCIL OF STATE OF EAST GERMANY

FRANCE -PIERRE MESSMER, PRIME MINISTER

CANADA - PRIME MINISTER - PIERRE TRUDEAU

CHINA - HEAD OF STATE - CHAIRMAN OF THE PEOPLE'S
REPUBLIC OF CHINA - MAO ZEDONG

PRESIDENT OF MEXICO PRESIDENT - LUIS ECHEVERRÍA

You Have Been Loved for

50 YEARS

Thats 600 months

2609 weeks | 18,262 days

438,291 hrs

26,297,460 MINUTES

1,576,800,000 seconds

and counting...

Cost of living 1972

Average House £4,800

In today's money that's approx £72,000

Average Salary £1,300

In today's money that's approx £19,000

Average Car price £1,200

In today's money that's approx £19,000

Gallon of petrol £0.38

In today's money that's approx £6

A dozen eggs £0.25	£3.90 in today's money
Loaf of Bread £0.10	£1.56 in today's money
2lb Sugar £0.10	£1.56 in today's money
12oz Kellogs cornflakes £0.11	£1.72 in today's money
1pt Milk £0.05	£0.78 in today's money
400g Bacon £0.34	£5.31 in today's money
Stork margarine 6 1/2p	£1.01 in today's money
8oz Nescafe coffee £0.47	£7.34 in today's money
Daily Mirror Newspaper 2.5-3p	£0.43 in today's money

DID YOU KNOW?

Not only did Monty Python give the World amazing comedy, they also contributed towards our British vernacular giving us the popular term 'spam'. It comes from a 1972 sketch set in a restaurant. 2 customers peruse the menu, and find everything on the menu contains spam. The relevance comes from the connection that regardless of what you want, you cannot get away from spam.

A sudden and random set of explosions of sea mines off the coast of Vietnam (1972) was finally explained when in 2018, technology provided the information that a massive Solar Storm would have triggered the magnetic sensors on the mines.

Shoichi Yokoi (a Japanese soldier) was found on the Island of Guam in 1972. It transpired he had spent 28 years in the jungle. He was the third last soldier to surrender after the end of the 2nd World War.

The rumour that Walt Disney was cryogenically frozen was widely reported in the news from 1966 onwards. In 1972, these speculations were put to bed when his daughter made a public statement to confirm that her father did not wish to be frozen and said "I doubt my father had even heard of cryonics."

Vesna Vulovic fell 10,160m from JAT Flight 367 when a bomb -concealed in a briefcase- exploded killing everyone on the flight except her. She fell without a parachute and her survival made her a world record holder for survival of the highest fall without a parachute.

10 MOST POPULAR BABY NAMES 1972

JENNIFER	MICHAEL
MICHELLE	CHRISTOPHER
LISA	JAMES
KIMBERLY	DAVID
AMY	JOHN
ANGELA	ROBERT
MELISSA	JASON
STEPHANIE	BRIAN
HEATHER	WILLIAM
NICOLE	MATTHEW

50 & FAMOUS

- **DWAYNE JOHNSON** MAY 2ND ACTOR

- **BEN AFFLECK** AUGUST 15TH ACTOR

- **CAMERON DIAZ** AUGUST 30TH ACTRESS

- **GWYNETH PALTROW** SEPTEMBER 27TH

- **EMINEM** OCTOBER 17TH RAPPER

- **IDRIS ELBA** SEPTEMBER 6TH ACTOR

- **BILLIE JOE ARMSTRONG** FEBRUARY 17TH SINGER

- **JENNIFER GARNER** APRIL 17TH ACTRESS

- **NOTORIOUS B.I.G** 21ST MAY RAPPER

- **SHAQUILLE O'NEAL** MAR 6TH NBA STAR

Music

'70s Music

When you think of the '70s it's impossible not to envisage Glam Rock. In direct contrast with the dreary and depressing political, social & economic landscape, Glam Rock gave the world some sparkle. 3 main figures come to mind as icons of Glam - T-Rex, David Bowie & Elton John. The music of the '70s flourished with colour, style & excessive personality. This revolt against the 'norm' also saw the birth of the Punk movement. This came later on in the '70s of which arguably the most well known is the Sex Pistols. Britain was awash with different music scenes vibrant, loud and not willing to fade into the background and accept their 'lot'.

1970 Edison Lighthouse

1971 T Rex

1972 The New Seekers

1973 Slade

1974 Abba

1975 David Bowie

1976 Abba

1977 Donna Summer

1978 Boomtown Rats

1972 No1 Hits

What was the number 1 hit when you were born?

Check out the list below to find out.

1st Jan – T.Rex   'Electric Warrior'

8th Jan – The New Seekers   'I'D like to Teach the World to Sing'

5th Feb – T.Rex   'Telegram Sm'

19th Feb – Chicory Tip   'Son of my Father'

11th March – Nilsson   'Without You'

15th April – The Pipes and the Drums   'Amazing Grace'

20th May – T.Rex   'Metal Guru'

17th June – Don McLean   'Vincent'

1st July – Slade   Take me Back 'Ome'

8th July – Donny   'Osmond Puppy Love'

12th August   Alice Cooper   'Schools out'

2nd September – Rod Stewart   'You Wear it Well'

9th September – Slade   'Mama Weer All Crazy Now'

30th September – David Cassidy   'How can I be Sure'

14th Oct – Lieutenant Pigeon   'Mouldy Old Dough'

11th Nov – Gilbert O'Sullivan   'Clair'

25th Nov – Chuck Berry   'My Ding-a-Ling'

23rd Dec – Jimmy Osmond

'Long Haired Lover from Liverpool'

Marc Bolan; born Mark Feld; 30) died 1977
Marc had many strings to his bow but was most famously Lead singer of the band T.Rex and was one of the pioneers of glam rock.

British rock group Mungo Jerry enjoyed success in the early 1970s, The group's name was inspired by the poem "Mungojerrie and Rumpleteazer", by T.S Elliot

Their biggest and most widely known hit was "In the Summertime".

Sir Roderick David Stewart CBE

Rod Stewart is one of the best-selling music artist all time, having sold over 250 million records worldwide.

- 10 No.1 albums
- 31 top ten single hits
- 6 No.1 hits

He was knighted in the 2016 Birthday Honours for services to music and charity.

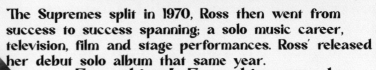

The Supremes split in 1970, Ross then went from success to success spanning; a solo music career, television, film and stage performances. Ross' released her debut solo album that same year. Everything Is Everything, gave her, her first UK number-one single "I'm Still Waiting".

She then dominated the world with her spectacular globe trotting sell out concert tours.

Albums - she enjoyed hit after hit with Touch Me in the Morning (1973), Mahogany (1975) and Diana Ross (1976) and their number-one hit singles, "Touch Me in the Morning", "Theme from Mahogany" and "Love Hangover", respectively. Ross further released numerous top-ten hits Throughout the 70s and into the decades that followed.

TRANSPORT

The era of commercial flights began was back in 1970 when the first Pan Am Boeing Jet landed at Heathrow. With that first flight the status of flying began to change as more 'ordinary' families could afford to take trips abroad. Suddenly it was realistic to travel all over the world, a thing that was unthinkable to most people. British holidays before this were still very much a seaside trip or Butlins resort if you were lucky.

Almost everything in the '70s was influenced by new technology in one way or another. For transport we saw some spectacular achievements in technology with the invention of the fastest passenger aircraft in the world, Concorde. Concorde first flew in service from 1976, built by Britain & France it was a real engineering feat. Flying at 2.100 kilometres per hour. Concorde flew between 1976-2003. It retired partly due to the fact it was hugely uneconomical with fares very few in the World could afford. Originally it cost £431 to fly Concorde between London and Washington.

Today there are approx 39 million cars on the road. Back in 1971 that figure was nearer 13 million at just a third of todays licensed cars. The infrastructure however has not expanded at the same rate. In 2018 there was 246,700 miles of road in total, up less than a quarter form the figure of 203,400 miles in 1971.

The top four car manufacturers all released new cars at the turn of the decade. Ford Escort was among the new versions, originally launched in 1967. You will also of course remember the Ford Capri which is credited with bringing sports car

Top ten selling cars of the '70s

1. Ford Cortina
2. Ford Escort
3. Mini
4. Morris Marina
5. Vauxhall Viva
6. Austin/Morris 1100/1300
7. Austin Allegro
8. Ford Capri
9. Hillman Avenger
10. Austin Maxi

CHANGING TRENDS

Between the 1890s and the 1930s walking was the most common form of getting to work and it remained the main means of commuting for one-third to one-fifth of the population in smaller towns and cities as late as the 1970s. After 1950 the use bicycles declined as other forms of transport became available. This decline was continuous to the mid-1970s, when it levelled off, and usage has remained fairly consistent ever since.

FORD ESCORT

From your Mercury dealer

List : $8.50 (each kit) Plus tax   List : $7.80 (each kit) Plus tax   List : $26.00 each. Plus tax

e your Ford Dealer for these new accessory releases Ford

BRITISH LEYLAND build a car to suit your requirements. Check the model specification chart at the front of this booklet and see which car most nearly fits your own individual needs.

Films

Diamonds are Forever

Due to the cost of Sean Connery's extortionate fee, the special effects budget had to be significantly reduced. He was paid a whopping $1,250,000 to play James Bond.

A Clockwork Orange

The scene when the character Alex, performs 'Singing in the rain' while he attacks his victims was unscripted. Stanley Kubrick reportedly spend a full four days playing around with this scene. The rights to 'Singing in the rain' cost the director $10,000.

The Godfather

The cat seen in the scenes in Vito's study was actually a stray that had appeared on the set, Copploa took the cat to Brando and told him to improvise with it through the scenes, they bonded so much the cat sat in his lap during takes for the whole day

Films 1972

- **THE GODFATHER** DIRECTED BY FRANCIS FORD COPPOLA. STARRING MARLON BRANDO, AL PACINO, JAMES CAAN

- **STEPTOE & SON** DIRECTED BY CLIFF OWEN, STARRING WILFRID BRAMBELL, HARRY H CORBETT, CAROLY SEYMOUR

- **DIAMONDS ARE FOREVER** DIRECTED BY GUY HAMILTON. STARRING SEAN CONNORY, JILL ST.JOHN, CHARLES GRAY, LANA WOOD, JIMMY DEAN & BRUCE CABOT

- **FIDDLER ON THE ROOF** DIRECTED BY NORMAN JEWISON, STARRING TOPOL, NORMA CRANE, LEONARD FREY, MOLLY PICON & PAUL MANN

- **THE FRENCH CONNECTION** DIRECTED BY WILLIAM FRIEDKIN, STARRING GENE HACKMAN, ROY SCHEIDER, FERNANDO REY

- **NICHOLAS AND ALEXANDER** DIRECTED BY FRANKLIN J. SCHAFFNER, STARRING MICHAEL JAYTON, JANET SUZMAN, RODERIC NOBLE

- **STRAW DOGS** DIRECTED BY SAM PECKINPAH, STARRING DUSTIN HOFFMAN, SUSAN GEORGE, PETER VAUGHAN

- **RYAN'S DAUGHTER** DIRECTED BY DAVID LEAN, STARRING ROBERT MITCHUM, TREVOR HOWARD JOHN MILLS

- **WHATS UP DOC** DIRECTED BY PETER BOGDANOVICH. STARRING BARBRA STEISAND, RYAN ONEAL, MADELINE KAHN

- **DIRTY HARRY** DIRECTED BY DON SIEGEL. STARRING CLINT EASTWOOD, ANDY ROBINSON, HARRY GUARDINO, RENI SATONI & JOHN VERNON

- **SHAFT** DIRECTED BY GORDON PARKS, STARRING RICHARD ROUNDTREE, MOSES GUNN, CHARLES CIOFFI

- **A CLOCKWORK ORANGE** DIRECTED BY STANLEY KUBRICK, STARRING MALCOLM MCDOWELL, PATRICK MAGEE, MICHAE; BATES

Popular '70s TV Shows

1971 – 91% of families had a TV

The early 1970s saw a focus on comedy shows. ITV were the clear leaders of this with the exception of BBC's Steptoe and Son. The BBC set their sights on taking the comedy mantle and by the mid '70s they had made real progress. They then made some classic comedy shows that are still enjoyed today; Faulty Towers (1975) and 'The Good Life'(1975). By the end of the '70s the BBC had overtaken ITV producing the best and most popular shows on TV.While you were too young to watch them at the time of release you'll no doubt see a few favourites. Many still shown as repeats on TV today.

The big news of the decade? You could watch in colour! By the end of the '60s 3 of the main stations began broadcasting in colour.

ARE YOU BEING SERVED?
UK (BBC) Situation Comedy. BBC 1 1973-9; 1981; 1983; 1985
ANTIQUES ROADSHOW UK (BBC) Antiques. BBC 1 1979-
ALL CREATURES GREAT AND SMALL
UK (BBC) Drama. BBC 1 1978-80; 1983; 1985;1988-90
THE BENNY HILL SHOW
UK (BBC) Comedy. BBC 1 1955-1968; Thames 1969-89
BLAKE'S 7 UK (BBC) Science Fiction. BBC 1 1978-81
BLESS THIS HOUSE
UK (Thames) Situation Comedy. ITV 1971-4, 1976
CALLAN UK (ABC/Thames) Secret Agent Drama. ITV 967-72
CILLA UK (BBC) Variety. BBC 1
CORONATION STREET
UK (Granada) Drama. ITV 1960-present day
CROSSROADS
UK (ATV/Central/Carlton) Drama. ITV 1964-88; ITV 1 2001-3
DAD'S ARMY UK (BBC) Situation Comedy. BBC 1 1968-77
DOCTOR WHO UK (BBC) Science Fiction. BBC 1 1963-89
THE DES O'CONNOR SHOW UK (ATV) Comedy.
FAWLTY TOWERS UK (BBC). Situation Comedy. BBC 2 1975; 1979
THE GENERATION GAME
UK (BBC) Game Show. BBC 1 1971-82; 1990- 2002
GEORGE AND MILDRED UK (Thames) Situation Comedy) 1976-9
THE GOOD LIFE UK (BBC). Situation Comedy. BBC 1 1975-8
GRANGE HILLUK (BBC/Mersey), Children's Drama. BBC 1978-
LAST OF THE SUMMER WINEUK (BBC) Situation Comedy. BBC 1 1973; 1975-6; 1978-9; 1981-93; 1995-
PLEASE SIR!UK (LWT) Situation Comedy. ITV 1968-72
MORCAMBE AND WISE UK (ATV) Comedy. 1961-7; BBC 1 1968-76; ITV 978-84
MONTY PYTHON'S FLYING CIRCUS
UK (BBC) Comedy. BBC 1 1969-73; BBC 2 1973
OPPORTUNITY KNOCKS UK (Associated Rediffusion/ ABC/Thames/BBC) Talent Show. ITV 1956-78; BBC 1 1987-90
PRISONER: CELL BLOCK H
Australia (Grundy) Drama. ITV 1979-87
SOME MOTHERS DO 'AVE 'EM
UK (BBC) Situation Comedy. BBC 1 1973-5; 1978
STEPTOE AND SON
UK (BBC) Situation Comedy. BBC 1 1962-5; 1970; 1972-4
THE SWEENEY
UK (Euston Films/Thames) Police Drama. ITV 975-6; 1978
THIS IS YOUR LIFE UK (BBC/Thames) Entertainment. BBC 1955- 4; ITV 1969-94; BBC 1 1994-2003
TOP GEAR UK (BBC) Motoring Magazine. BBC 2 1978-
THE TWO RONNIES UK (BBC) Comedy. BBC 1/BBC 2 1

Adverts in the '70s

During the '70s more houses than ever owned a colour TV, with more than one channel. This gave people more choice than they ever had before. The result of this changed the way products were marketed and Brands were quick to take advantage of this new opportunity. Where traditionally they would have primarily advertised in newspapers and magazines, more brands were turning towards the Television. This shift gave consumers more power -if they didn't like the advertising they saw they would switch over- and led to a consumer based approach as opposed the the existing product centric philosophy.

At the beginning of the decade ads were still fairly product centred however the recognition of the need to appeal to customers and to communicate the reasons why their product was the best led to Brands digging deep into the narrative of why people should buy their brand over another. Comparison ads are the result of this and are still seen in advertising today. The most obvious examples being Burger King and McDonalds, Pepsi Vs Coca-cola.

The advert for Mothercare on the following page showing another early example "See how much more your money buys at Mothercare..." Showing not just the benefits of the products but looking at the value as opposed to other brands available. The '70s advertising world became subject to more rules & regulations that previous decades. Brands no longer had the same elastic approach to listing the benefits of their products. Regulations meant that a more honest approach was required and this in turn increased consumer confidence. The PLJ lemon juice advert on the following page shows it wasn't quite as strict as the regulations we have in place now. The clear message is that this miracle juice will help you lose weight, be beautiful and have great skin.

The advances in technology allowed companies to start collecting more information about their consumers. For the first time companies were collecting data to help them focus their advertising, information on demographics, analysing consumers spending behaviours, creating projections based on analysis of previous data all of which fed into the campaigns to create more demand for their Brand/product. Another change within advertising is in the emphasis on emotional approaches. This led to adverts which we would now find offensive and certainly wouldn't be shown on our screens. Sexual innuendo being one of the main culprits, that shows us how different the accepted culture was just 5 decades ago.

Adverts shown on TV in the '70s were dominated by food brands and soap powder brands. The adverts on the following double page are all original adverts from the '70s. You might also remember the Smash martians? OXO sent 'Katie' - who had appeared in ads for OXO since the 50s- to America to explain the wonderful cooking aid to her American friends. This gave the brand added glamour! **HP Fruity Sauce,** the original HP sauce was made in 1903. Fruity sauce was developed in 1969 to offer a milder alternative to the original sauce. Did you know the HP stands for Houses of Parliament? The original recipe was invented by Frederick Gibson Garter, a grocer from Nottingham. He sold the recipe for £150 to settle a debt with Edwin Samson Moore, the founder of the midlands vinegar company, who launched it as HP sauce.

Coffee mate - magazine advert 1972. The product developed in 1961 was particularly popular throughout the '70s.

Babybel - the company was started by Joules Bel in 1865. This long established brand continues it's success today with over 2 billion pieces of cheese sold each year (that's a staggering 4 thousand cheeses munched every minute!).

Ceylon tea & PG Tips- it wasn't until the 1970s that tea companies were selling tea bags as opposed to loose leaf tea. Teabags were sold from earlier in the Century but they didn't catch on until the '70s. Advertising helped drive this change in consumption.

Old Spice - a Christmas advert showing various gift sets. It's highly likely your Dad would have received a few of these through the 70's along with some patterned socks.

Vencat Curry powder - curry was a dish that previous to the 1970s was unheard of. Original adverts came with recipe suggestions as it was still an ingredient most housewives were unsure of.

Hoover Gas fire, The Show-off- 1970 advert. Although gas fires were in households from as early as the '40s, due to the post war austerity they were not commonplace until the '60s and even then often used sparingly. Through advertising, the convenience of gas fires ensured that from the '70s these became increasingly popular as real coal fires became obsolete.

Coal Tar Soap - created by William Valentine Wright in 1860, Wrights coal tar soap was a popular brand of soap in many households. The soap can still be bought today to treat various skin disorders.

Fashion 1970s

As the Swinging Sixties gave way to the 1970s, the accessibility of fashion had turned a corner. The boutique shops excelled in creating individual styles that reflected the various movements of the era.

The emergence of new technologies heavily impacted the fashion industry. The main influence being the new fabrics that were cheaply available through mass production. The '70s is sometimes referred to as the 'Polyester decade' - the material new on the market was embraced with wild abandon. The fact it was cheap, and didn't allow any air to permeate didn't seem to bother anyone at the time.

The silhouette of the '70s for men and women was typically a tight fitted top and wide bell bottom trousers. You may well be able to look back at some spectacular flares with platform shoes featured in the family photo album!

The 1970s was all about a move to Individualism. This was a move away from the community spirit prevalent in the '60s.

Music influenced fashion, fashion influenced music, individuals felt free to experiment with non conformist styles. This impacted the fashion industry overall as here we see the beginnings of a much more casual approach through mainstream society.

Have you heard of the Peacock revolution?

You would have been too young to be part of this but perhaps an older sibling or family member participated in strutting about the town in ruffled lacy shirts, with lace on the cuffs and the neckline. Hence the name Peacock revolution - It was a sight to behold.

Designer Eyewear

Butterick 4139 $1.25 Canada $1.55
SIZE 28
RETURNABLE

1970s Fashion

Marks & Spencers advertising from a 1970s edition of Woman & Home. The article looks at the dilemma of what to wear in the workplace now that more and more women continued working after marriage. Throughout the '70s trouser suits for women grew in popularity.

Children's wear followed adult fashion with bright colours, patterns, stripes and a continuation of knitwear and crochet.

You can see from these adverts the fashion styles still looked to the past taking influences from the 60's and further back to the '30s & '40s. Designers used details from the past with innovation in new fabrics to produce modern fashion styles.

'70s Toys

As a child of the '70s you'll remember the classics such as Chopper bikes, roller skates, space hoppers and the arrival of the Atari computer in '79. Take a trip back and reminisce about other popular '70s toys.

1970 Toy of the year goes to Sindy doll. Supermarkets begin selling toys. The must have Christmas toy was the Neon Nerf Ball (which cost £1.25).

1971 Toy of the year is awarded to Katie Kopycat. We also see the arrival of the infamous Spacehopper and the beginning of the Clackers craze. No1 on Santas toy list - the Mastermind Board game which cost a whopping £1.64.

1972 Plasticraft modelling kit wins the coveted Toy of the Year. Feature in Toy Trader forecasts Leisuredromes - theme park shopping centres. Christmas must have - Uno card game (cost £1.01)

1973 A new category in the retail awards - game of the year - is won by Invicta's Mastermind. The industrial & economic issues cause a shortage of plastic which causes issue for toy manufacturers. Children's pocket money averages 9p. New dolls this year include Chelsea Girl and Daisy. Christmas must have - Shrinky Dinks; large sheets of pre-painted colours or shapes that were shrunk in a heated oven.

1974 Lego wins its first Toy of the Year. The 3 day week badly affects trade. Big hits of the year include boxing toy Raving Bonkers, Denys Fisher Potter's Wheel and game Lexidata. Christmas must have - Dungeons & Dragons fantasy table top role playing game (cost £3.69)

1975 Lego wins Toy of the year again. Monopoly celebrates the big 40. Cluedo is a relatively young 25 and womblemania hits Britain. You'd have been 4 so may well remember singing along to the theme tune! Christmas must have - Othello strategy board game (cost £2.76).

1976 Peter Powell Kites wins Toy of the Year as kites enjoyed a renewed popularity. Meccano is 75 years old, and Mattel sets up in the UK. Flop of the year was Streaker, A toy that was supposed to parody the success of the yo-yo and the hula-hoop. Christmas must have toy - Magna Doodle (cost £2.63 - still selling today).

1977 Playpeople by Playmobil wins Toy of the Year award. Popular toys this year include: slime, Othello strategy board game & Holly Hobbie toys. Christmas must have - Star War figurines which cost £1.44 each.

1978 Toy of the Year goes to the Combine Harvester made by Britains. Chad Valley launches Huggy Bear - its first clinging bear.. A new range of Star wars toys make their debut. Omar Sharif launched board and card games at the Toy Fair at the NEC. Big hits this year included; Play-Doh Barber Shop - a true childhood classic, Star Wars Force Beams, Matchbox Powertrack, Mr Men and a new board game, Skirrid. Christmas must have was Hungry Hippos (cost £3.94).

1979 Legoland Space Sets wins Toy of the Year. Electronic games and sales of radio-controlled cars boom. New toys include Stop Boris (a creeping electronic spider stopped by a special gun). Christmas must have toy was the Strawberry Shortcake doll (cost £4.75). Of course other big news this year was the Atari computer.

Did you have one? Either way I'm sure you still remember the joy and wonder of your first game!

Do you remember?

Popular '70s Children's TV shows

The Wombles are furry creatures created by Elisabeth Beresford and originally appearing in a series of children's novels from 1968. The characters gained a higher national profile in the UK in the mid-1970s as a result of a BBC-commissioned children's tv show. It was made using stop-motion animation and the series became quite the hit. Womblemania hit the UK and a number of spin-off novelty songs hit the UK charts with success.

Animal Magic - a BBC kids TV series which ran from 1962 to 1983 from BBC Bristol. It began showing fortnightly then in 1964 was shown weekly.

Ivor the Engine a series originally made back in the 1958 in black & white, it enjoyed a revival when new shows were created in 1975 using new colour TV technology.

Brian Cant with Playaway. Brian Cant (12 July 1933 – 19 June 2017). Cant hosted or co-hosted the programmes Play Away (1971–84). Showing from your birth to your teens you will surely remember this!

Bleep and Booster - a children's cartoon series by William Timym (pronounced Tim) originally shown on the BBC's Blue Peter. A total of 313 five-minute episodes were released between 1964 and 1977.

Mr Benn – did you know you were sharing your special birthday year with Mr Benn? Created in 1971 by David McKee. The first episode was the Red Knight.

Crackerjack - aired on the BBC from 14 September 1955 until 21 December 1984 (except during your birth year 1971). A popular variety show for kids enjoyed by several generation over the 4 decades it ran.

The Clangers (BBC1 1969-1972) is a stop-motion animation children's tv series. The series is about a family of mouse-like creatures who live on a small moon-like planet. Conversing in a strange whistle like language and sustained with green soup & blue string pudding, made by the Soup Dragon.

Trumpton Fire Brigade

Chris Tarrant and Sally James on Tiswas

Bagpuss 13 episodes broadcast in 1974.

Roobarb & Custard

Captain Pugwash

Basil Brush

Rainbow

Banana Splits

Do you remember?

Songs from Television's Award Winning Childrens' Program

World Events

Copernicus Satellite

The OAO-3 Copernicus satellite is launched. This satellite was a research collaboration between the US and the UK. OAO-3 carried a UV telescope (made at Princeton) and an X-Ray experiment (created at the University of London). It was one of 4 missions, hailed as the most successful and led to many scientific discoveries. It remained in service until 1981.

Watergate Scandal

On the 17th June 1972, agents of the Nixon re-election campaign were arrested breaking into the office of the Democratic National Committee (Washing D.C Watergate complex). Investigation discovered that the re-election team had wiretapped the telephones in the office of Lawrence O'Brian (Democrat). The 5 operatives were arrested. President Nixon denied any knowledge but after investigations led by reporters at the Washington Post several damning facts confirmed his involvement and uncovers a campaign of political sabotage and spying. The investigation took place over 2 years and finally on the 8th August 1974 President Nixon announces he will resign the Presidency effective the next day. Vice President Gerald Ford issued Richard Nixon a full pardon, giving him immunity from prosecution from any crimes he had "committed or taken part in"

Smallpox The last major outbreak of smallpox in Europe breaks out in Yukoslavia.

US- Launches Landsat 1

NASA launches Landsat 1 Earth Resources Technology Satellite (ERTS) on 23rd July.

The satellite was designed as part of a suite of technology; the purpose was to observe Earth and provide detailed information for further study.

The satellite transmitted over 300,000 images of Earth surface before it became obsolete just 6 years later.

Space - Pioneer 10

3rd March 1972, saw NASA launch the first spacecraft to travel through the asteroid belt and the very first to visit Jupiter. The mission was a success, Pioneer 10 landed on Jupiter in December of 1973 and was able to transmit images of the largest plant in the Solar System. It is a long serving spacecraft - the mission finally complete in 1997.

XI Winter Olympics - Japan

1006 athletes from 35 different countries participated in the games, held between 3rd February-13th 1972. The Japanese government spent enormous sums of money investing in new infrastructure. In preparation for the games.

UK - Miners Strike

The National Executive Committee of NUM reject a pay rise offer sparking the first miners strike since 1926. Miners picket coal power stations and eventually move to all power stations. On the 9th February the British Government declare a state of Emergency; a 3 day week is announced to save electricity. Later in the month an agreement is reached between NUC and the Government and the workers return to their posts.

US - Equal rights Amendment is passed by US Senate on the 22nd March providing legal equality of the sexes .

Anti-Ballistic Missile Treaty 1972

Talks take place during May 1972, the United States and Soviet Union sign the Anti-Ballistic Missile (ABM) Treaty. US President Richard Nixon and Soviet Premier Leonid Brezhev met in Moscow to negotiate arms control. The ABM Treaty limited both countries to 2 anti-ballistic missile complexes with a further limit of 100 missiles each. It was a historic moment, in that it was the first time a US president had walked on Soviet soil since World War II.

Vietnam 1972

Last US troops withdrawn from Vietnam.

Apollo 17 lands on the moon and the last men to walk on the moon are Harrison Schmitt & Eugene Cernan

1972 UK Events

Jan - The first Uk female judge was appointed. Rose Heilbron who pioneered many firsts for women in the 70s UK sat at the Old Bailey.

The coal miners strike action began on the 9th Feb and lasted for over seven weeks.

30th Jan - 'Bloody Sunday' in Northern Ireland. Fourteen people were tragically killed by British Troops while demonstrating in Derry.

2nd Feb - the British Embassy in Dublin is burned down in protest of the killing of 14 people on the 30th January.

3rd-13th Feb - Winter Olympics in Japan. Neither Britain nor Northern Ireland won any medals in the games.

9th Feb- The British Government declare a state of emergency due to the miners strike. A 3 day working week is announced to save electricity.

March - Ford Cars promote new Granada model., To be built in the Dagenham plant.

March - CND organise a protest against the Nuclear base at Aldermaston.

30th March - Parliament of Northern Ireland is suspended.

3rd May - the first UEFA Cup Final . Tottenham Hotspur beat Wolverhampton Wanderers 2-1

6th May - Leeds United won the FA Cup.

The courts of Assize and Quarter sessions in England and Wales are replaced with the Courts Act 1971. It is also

1st July - The first official gay pride march in London.

9 August – Musical Jesus Christ Superstar made its West End debut.

26th August-10th Sep - Munich Olympics. Britain * Northern Ireland take home 4 Gold, 5 silver & 10 Bronze.

1st Sep - the legal age to leave school is increased from 15yr to 16 yrs old.

11 September – Mastermind broadcast for the first time.

12th Sep - 2 British trawlers were sunk by Icelandic gunboat triggering the second cod war between Iceland and the UK.

13th September - the first Hypermarkets opens in the UK. Carrefour opens in South Wales.

16th October – Emmerdale Farm first aired.

October - Cambridge changes male only policy to allow entrance to female students.

November - The PEOPLE party were formed (predecessor of the Green Party) they were the first political party to have their policies focused on green politics.

Dec 10th - Nobel prize for economics goes to John Hicks for "pioneering contributions to general economic equilibrium theory and welfare theory."

1972 - marriage rates peak

1972 - British car production peaks at almost 2 million units.

1972 - Honda begin to import cars following the success of their motorcycles. The first car to be imported was the small civic hatchback.

'70s Inventions

1972

World's first electronic digital wristwatch is introduced by Hamilton. The retail price is $2,100, that's over $12K today.

Floppy Disk 1971

A small team of engineers at IBM were working on developing a reliable system for loading instructions and data transfers to mainframe computers created the first floppies on the market. IBM began selling floppies in 1971. It wasn't until 1972 they received a patent and then the real success came when Apple released Apple II with 5 inch floppy disk. This allowed the general public to easily transfer data and load systems to their PCs at home.

John Blakenbaker, while working at Kenbar Corporation in 1970, invented what is widely considered to be the worlds first personal computer. The Kenbak-I was released in early 1971.

Sony Walkman 1979

The invention of this technology shaped culture throughout the 80's. It changed the way young people could listen to music. The walkman took the world by storm when it entered the market in 1979. There aren't many people who were teenagers around the 80's that won't remember the joy of listening to a mixed tape on their walkman.

The Intel 4004 was the first microprocessor

Intel released the worlds first microprocessor in 1971. Stanley Mazor, Federico Faggin & Ted Holff co-inventors of the microprocessor received the National Medal of Technology and Innovation by US President Barack Obama.

'70s Inventions

Rubix Cube

Created by Erno Rubik (architecture professor) as a tool to teach his students about spatial relationships. This went on to become one of the most popular toys of the 80's. It remains a popular challenge today!

3M launched the product as 'Press 'n Peel' bookmark in stores in four cities in 1977, but results were disappointing. A year later, 3M instead issued free samples and rebranded to 'Post-Its' in 1979 when the rollout introduction began, and was sold across the United States from April 6, 1980. The following year, they were launched in Canada and Europe.

Pocket-sized electronic calculator Busicom LE-120A "HANDY", which was marketed early in 1971.

The first self contained digital camera was invented by an engineer at Kodak in 1975. Steven Sasson invented the camera which weighed 8lbs and took black & white photographs.

Mobile Phones

Modern day life seems impossible without our mobile phones. It's all thanks to Martin Cooper, senior engineer at Motorola who invented the technology in 1973.

Martin called a rival company (Bell laboratories) just to inform them they were speaking through a mobile phone. The first phones were enormous by today's standards.

The Motorola Dyna weighted 2.5lbs and was around 1/2ft in length. The charge time for a 30 min call was 10 hours.

Email 1971

As with mobile phones, emails have become an essential part of modern life. The first email was sent in 1971. Ray Tomlinson and Bolt Beranek developed text based technology that could send messages between computers through the ARPANET network using the @ symbol to route messages.

There is some debate over the true origin of the invention however as Shiva Ayyadurai claims that he built an electronic messaging platform in 1978. The young inventor was later awarded the copyright for "email".

Britain in the '70s

The '70s is widely reported as a time of hardship for many with a struggling economy, strikes, the winter of discontent and general uncertainty resulting in social and economic unrest.

It was a decade of constant strikes, primarily postal workers, miners and dustmen. The 3 day work week was imposed to help reduce the consumption of electricity. Introduced by the Conservative government to relieve the shortage caused by the 1973.74 oil crisis.

From 1st January 1974 commercial uses of electricity were limited to 3 day consecutive use with essential services such as hospitals and supermarkets deemed exempt. The economy was troubled by high rates of inflation, which then impacted on the unions as wages did not rise to meet inflation costs.

1977 saw mass celebration throughout Britain for the Queen's Silver Jubilee. The nation celebrated with street parties. While at the same time, a growing discontent in the legitimacy of a monarchy was brewing amongst many young people.

'God Save the Queen' a song by the Sex Pistols, was released in 1977 to coordinate with the Queens silver jubilee. This song reflected the mood of many young people finding frustration with their limited opportunities and displayed a rejection of the concept of a monarchy.

History was made when we elected our first female Prime Minister, Margaret Thatcher, in 1979.

Despite the bleak picture this paints, and the fact that upon discussion many people vividly remember the power cuts and scarcity of resources, the memories most shared are happy; filled with personal memories of happy childhoods, an ease of life that seems far from our fast paced technology crammed world of today.

It may well be the nostalgic effect with some rose tinted glasses thrown in for good measure. Memories of Bagpuss, space hoppers and playing all day in the streets with your friends tell a story of an idyllic childhood. However, it is true to say that behind the headlines, most ordinary families were actually better off than ever.

Munich Olympics 1972

26th AUGUST - 11TH SEPTEMBER

TOP 20 MEDAL TABLE WINNERS

	GOLD	SILVER	BRONZE
Soviet Union	50	27	22
United States	33	31	30
East Germany	20	23	23
West Germany	13	11	16
Japan	13	8	8
Australia	8	7	7
Poland	7	5	9
Hungary	6	13	16
Bulgaria	6	10	5
Italy	5	3	10
Sweden	4	6	6
Great Britain	4	5	9
cuba	3	1	4
Finland	3	1	4
Netherlands	3	1	1
France	2	4	7
Czechoslovakia	2	4	2
Kenya	2	3	4
Yugoslavia	2	1	2

The 1972 Summer Olympics, 'Die Heiteren Spilele'

The official title of the games was XX Olympiad. Held in Munich, Bavaria (26th Aug-11th Sep) these games were the 2nd Summer olympics to be held in Germany. The first time was in 1942 , held during the reign of Hitler and the Nazi regime. German people wanted these games to show the world that they were a democratic and optimistic society and hence nicknamed them 'Die Heiteren Spilele' translated as 'the cheerful games'.

The Olympic mascot was a dachshund 'Waldi', and was the first officially named mascot. The Soviet Union were the clear winners of the day. The Uk did not fare very well at all with no medals won.

The games were not the optimistic show that Germany hoped they would be, at no fault of their own. The Munich Massacre which saw eleven Israeli athletes and coaches and a West German police officer tragically murdered overshadowed the event.

Little Pips Press

Happy Birthday and here's to many more.

We hope you enjoyed reminiscing!

Our range of Birthday books includes all milestone years. Check out our range of other titles covering all the milestone birthdays from 40th-80th. We would love it if you could spend a few minutes to write a review on Amazon.

The legal stuff...

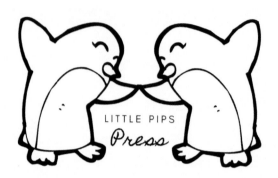

Attribution for photo images goes to the following talented photographers under the creative commons licenses specified:

Printed in Great Britain
by Amazon

12205324R00025